Tunes for Electronic Keyboard
Book 1

Nick Haines

CAMBRIDGE UNIVERSITY PRESS

Published by the Press Syndicate of the University of Cambridge
The Pitt Building, Trumpington Street, Cambridge CB2 1RP
40 West 20th Street, New York, NY 10011-4211, USA
10 Stamford Road, Oakleigh, Melbourne 3166, Australia

© Longman Group UK Limited 1989
© Cambridge University Press 1996

First published 1989 by Longman Group UK Limited
First published 1996 by Cambridge University Press, fifth printing

Printed in Great Britain by Bell and Bain Ltd, Glasgow

A catalogue record for this book is available from the British Library

Paperback: ISBN 0 521 56914 1

Notice to teachers
It is illegal to reproduce any part of this work in material form (including photocopying and electronic storage) except under the following circumstances:
(i) where you are abiding by a licence granted to your school or institution by the Copyright Licensing Agency;
(ii) where no such licence exists, or where you wish to exceed the terms of a licence, and you have gained the written permission of Cambridge University Press;
(iii) where you are allowed to reproduce without permission under the provisions of Chapter 3 of the Copyright, Designs and Patents Act 1988.

By the same author
Tunes for Electronic Keyboard Book 2
Start the Electronic Keyboard Books 1 and 2
Play the Electronic Keyboard Books 1 and 2
Composing at the Electronic Keyboard Books 1 and 2

Acknowledgements
We are grateful to the following for permission to reproduce copyright songs:

EMI Music Publishing Ltd and International Music Publications for 'Matchstalk men' words and music by Brian Burke and Michael Coleman © 1977 Great Northern Publishing Co. Ltd, London WC2 0LD; EMI Music Publishing Ltd, International Music Publications and Noel Gay Music for 'The sun has got his hat on' words by Ralph Butler, music by Noel Gay © 1932 Wests Ltd, administered by B. Feldman & Co. Ltd, London WC2H 0LD/EMI; Island Music Ltd for 'Sailing' by Gavin Sutherland © 1972 Island Music Ltd. All right reserved.

Contents

At the fair   2
Bobby Shaftoe   3
Skip to my lou   3
Baby Bossa   3
The whistling soldier   4
Silent night   4
Johnny Todd   5
Pastoral theme   5
Button Samba (duet)   6
The sun has got his hat on   8
Stewball   9
Matchstalk men and matchstalk cats and dogs   10
My bonnie lies over the ocean   12
Oranges and lemons   13
We wish you a Merry Christmas   13
Tom Dooley   13
Hurdy Gurdy   14
Swing low, sweet chariot   14
House of the rising sun   15
Ten green bottles   15
Three-note rocker   16
Santa Lucia   17
Sailing   18
Londonderry Air   19
Shortnin' bread   19
Toreador's song   20
Meaty Beaty   21
Silent movie   22
Blue note   22
Coppelia   23
In the hall of the Mountain King   24
Big Band Swinger   24
The Entertainer   26
Eine kleine Nachtmusik   28

Introduction

The tunes in this book have been arranged for use with the portable electronic keyboard. They are graded in difficulty and cover a wide range of style and technique. Most of the melodies can be played using the Single-finger chord selector found on all portable electronic keyboards. Some of the tunes, however, do require the Fingered-chord facility.

This sign indicates a fill-in bar. Press the fill-in button on your keyboard at the beginning of the bar and the automatic percussion will give you a bar's drum solo. If your keyboard has no fill-in facility, ignore this sign.

At the fair

Nick Haines

Bobby Shaftoe

The whistling soldier

Nick Haines

Silent night

Franz Grüber

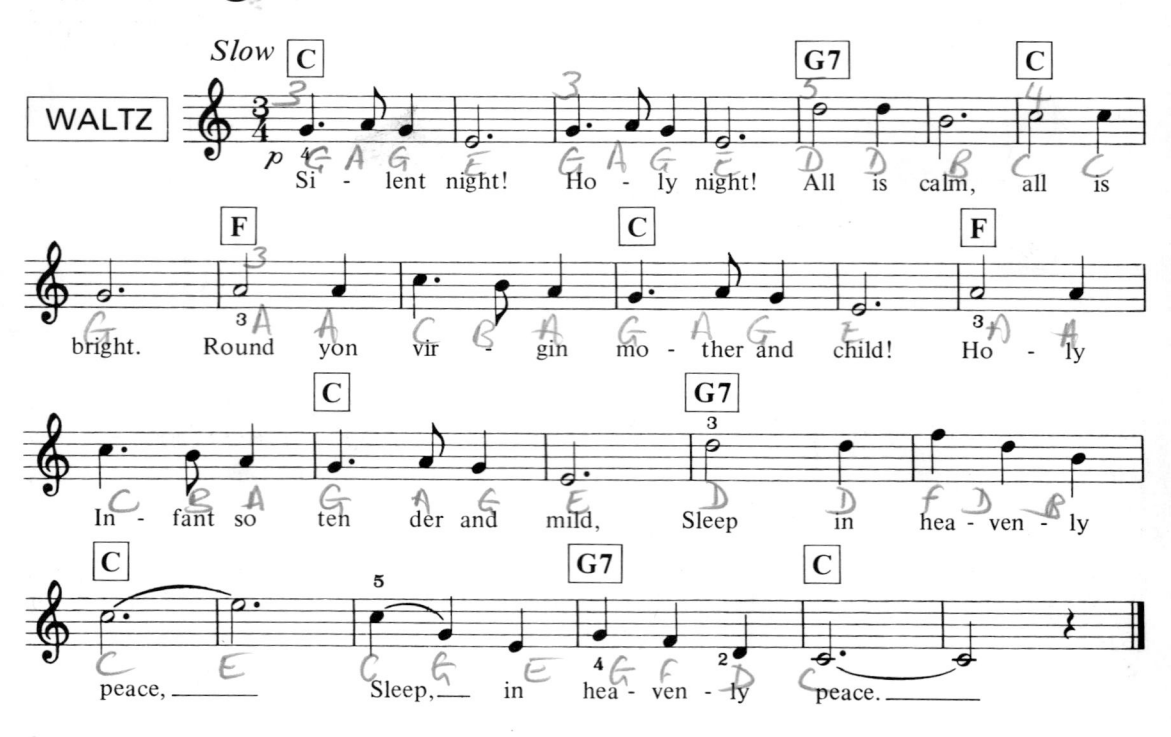

Johnny Todd

Traditional

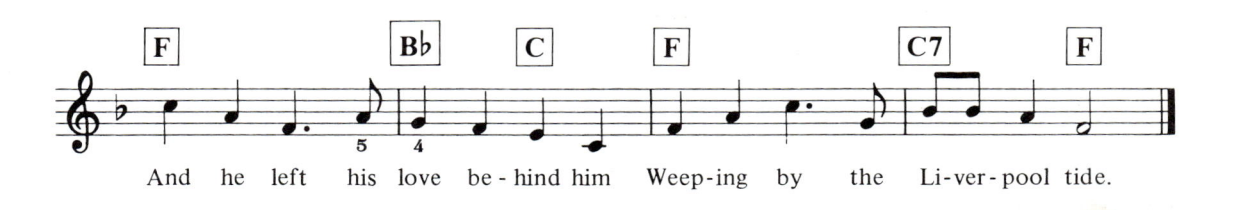

SWING

John-ny Todd he took a no-tion, For to cross the o-cean wide, And he left his love be-hind him Weep-ing by the Li-ver-pool tide.

Pastoral theme

Beethoven

* Switch the auto-chord off.

FLUTE

Button Samba

Nick Haines

Duet for two keyboards

If your Keyboard has a transposing switch, turn the control one position higher every time you see this sign ▲ .

7

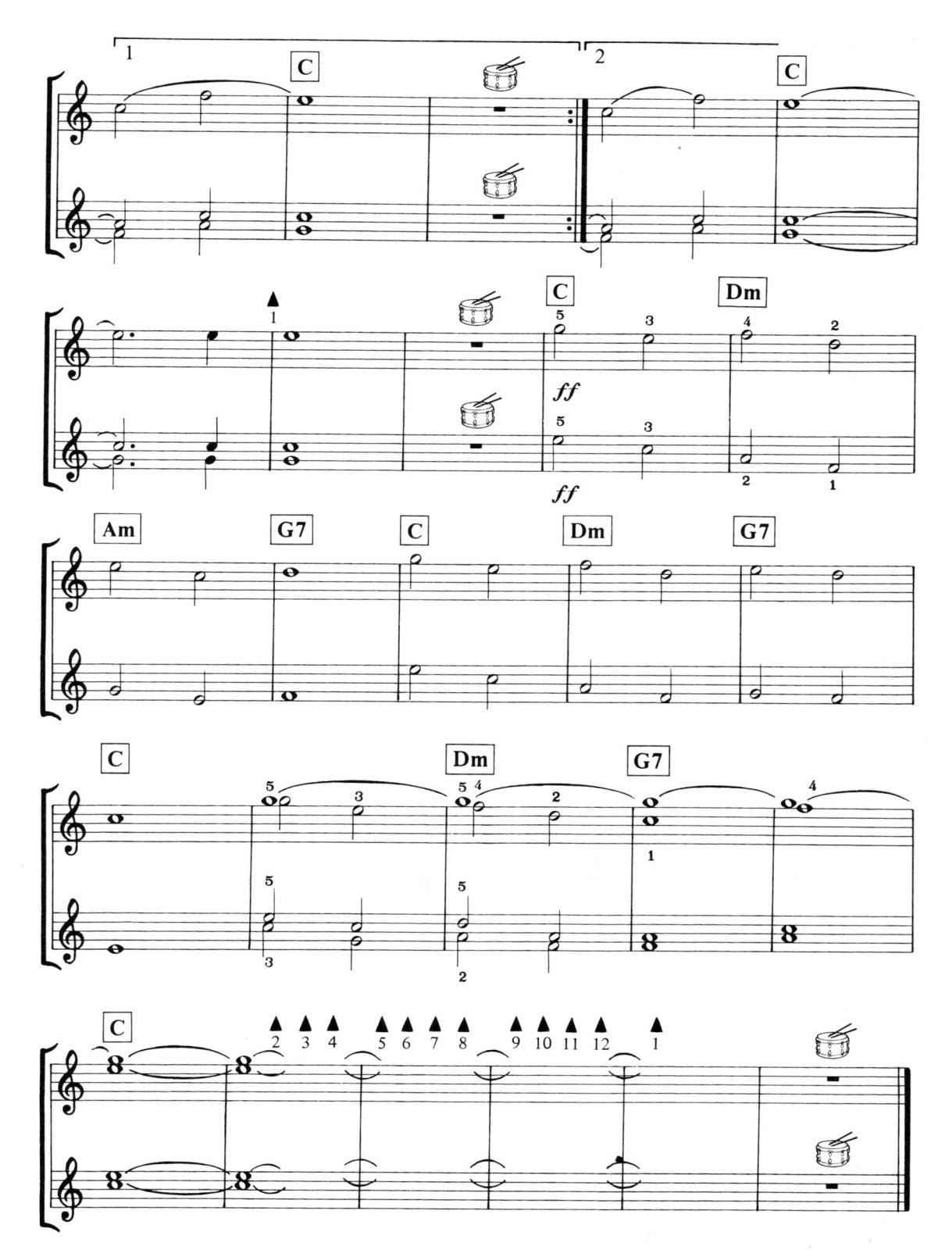

The sun has got his hat on

Words and music by
Ralph Butler and Noel Gay

Moderately

SWING

The sun has got his hat on, Hip - hip - hip - hoo -ray! The sun has got his hat on, and he's com - ing out to - day! Now we'll all be hap - py Hip - hip - hip - hoo -ray! The sun has got his hat on, and he's com - ing out to - day. He's been tan - ning tour - ists out in Tim - buc - too. Now he's com - ing back to do the same to

8

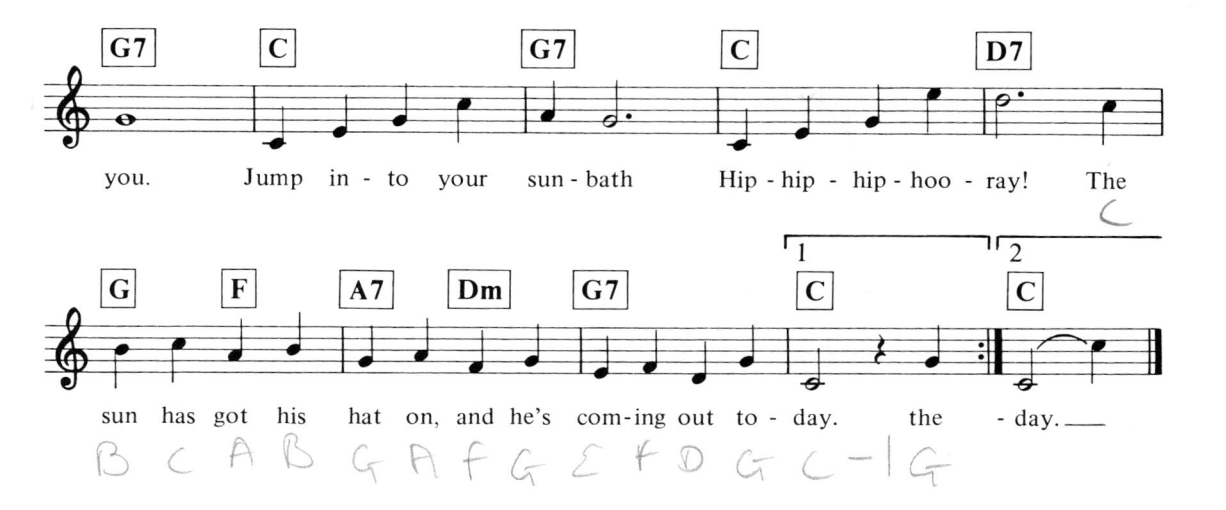

Stewball

Traditional

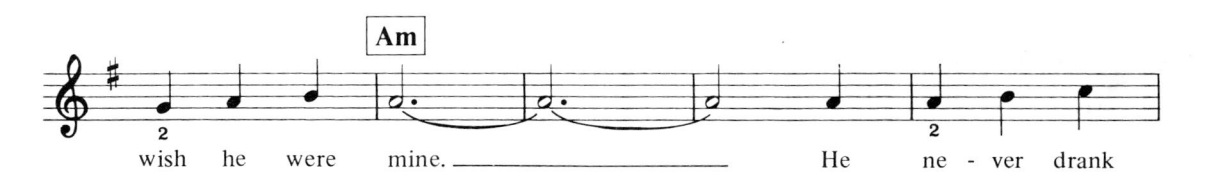

WALTZ

'Ol' Stewball was a race-horse, And I wish he were mine. He never drank water He always drank wine.

Matchstalk men and matchstalk cats and dogs

Words and music by
Michael Coleman and Brian Burke

G7 C Dm
And he paint - ed match - stalk men and match - stalk cats and dogs.
G7 C
He paint - ed kids on the cor - ner of the street that were spark - ing clogs.
Dm
Now he takes his brush and he waits out - side them fac - tory gates
G7 C
to paint his match - stalk men and match - stalk cats and dogs.

My bonnie lies over the ocean

Traditional English

Oranges and lemons

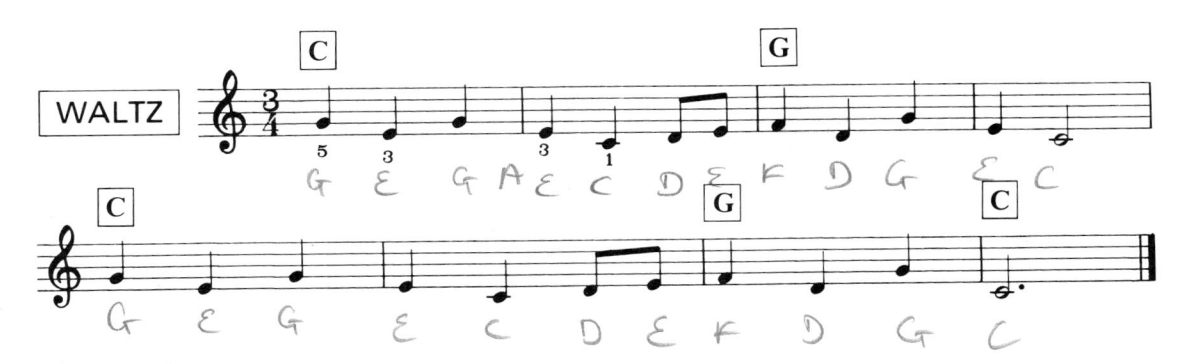

We wish you a merry Christmas

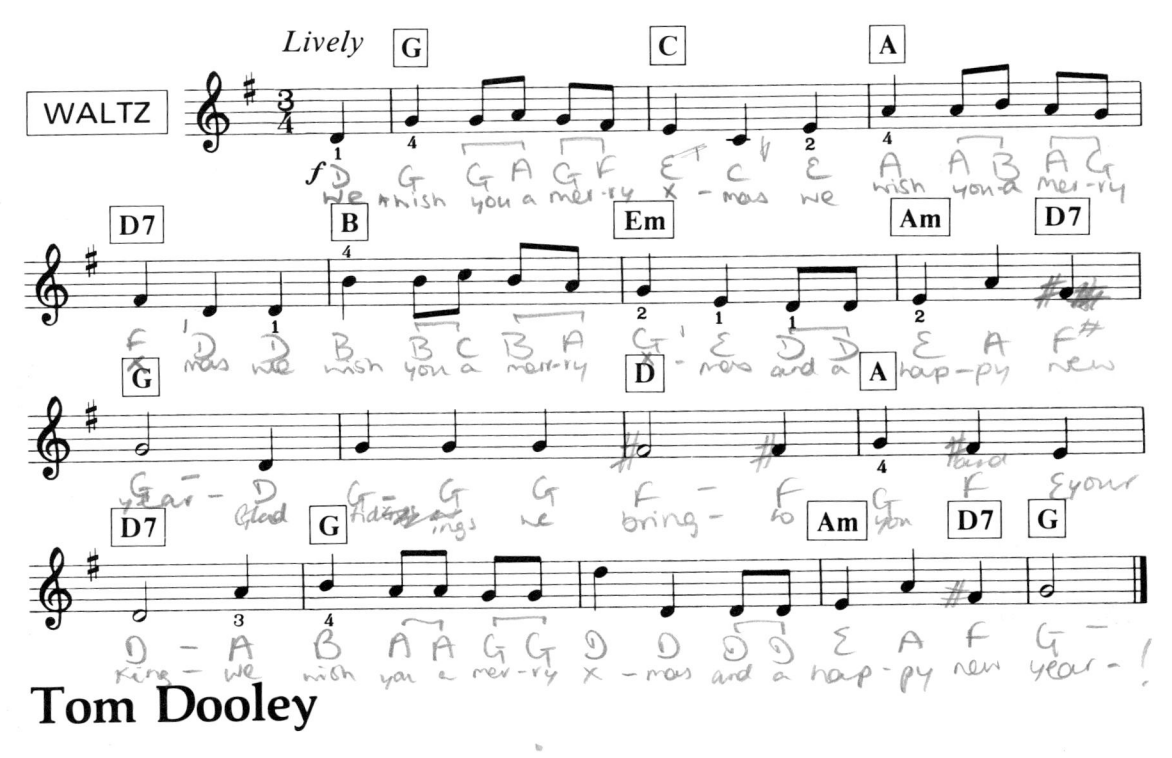

Tom Dooley

Hurdy Gurdy

Nick Haines

Swing low, sweet chariot

Spiritual

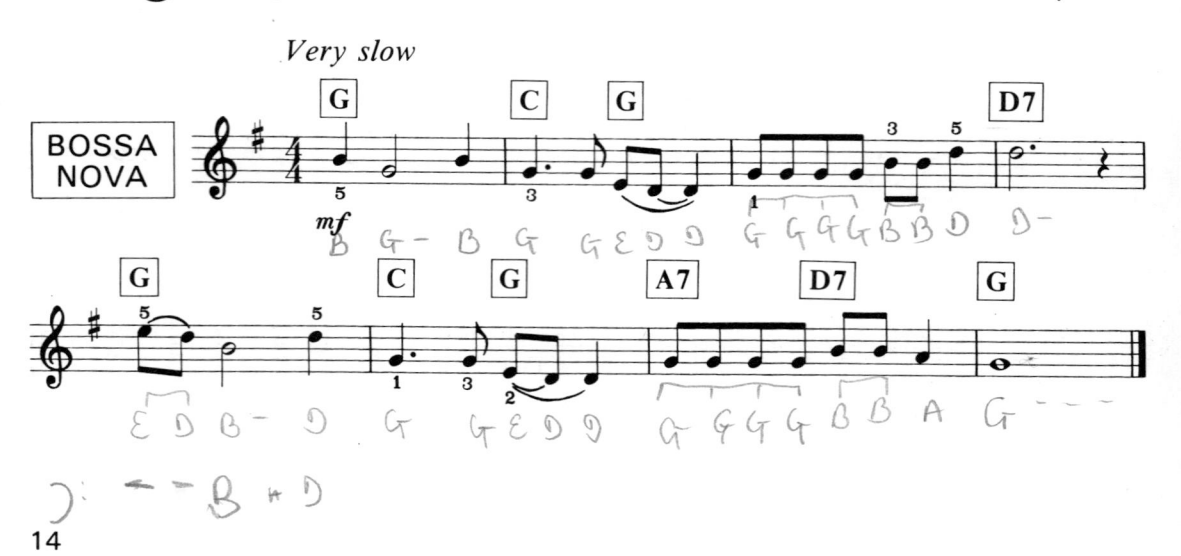

The House of the Rising Sun

Traditional

SLOW ROCK

There is a house in New Orleans, they call the Ri-sing Sun. And it's been the ru-in of many a poor boy, and God, I know I'm one.

There

Ten green bottles

SWING

Ten green bot-tles hang-ing on the wall Ten green bot-tles hang-ing on the wall And if one green bot-tle should ac-ci-dent'ly fall, there'd be nine green bot-tles hang-ing on the wall.

15

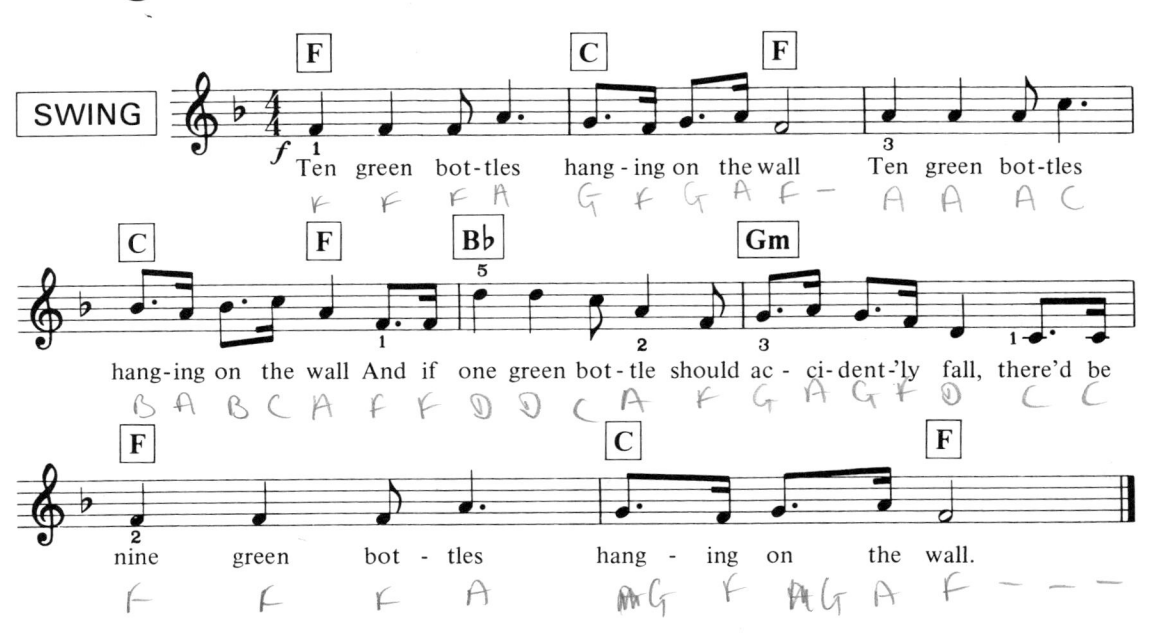

Three-note rocker

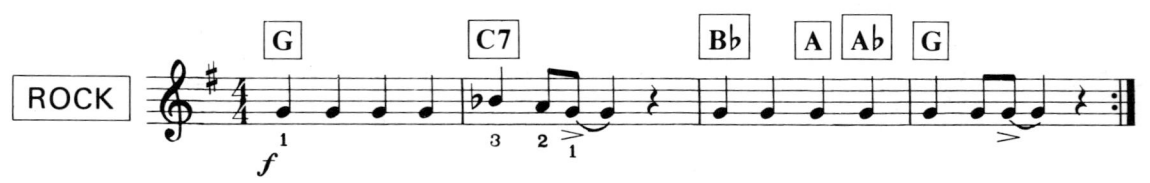

Nick Haines

Santa Lucia

Neapolitan Song

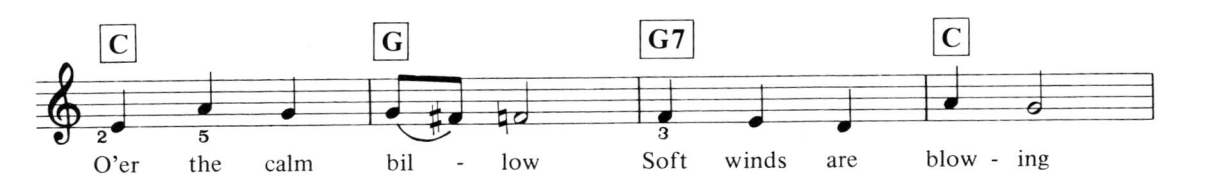

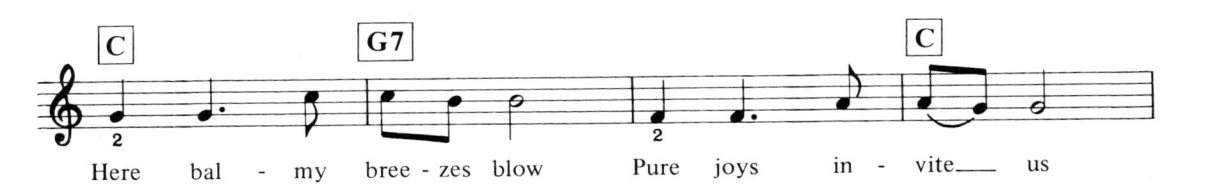

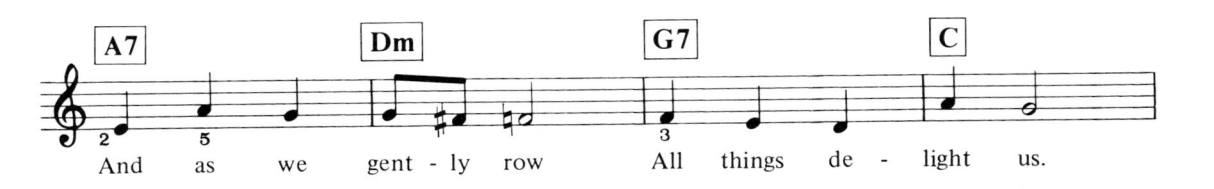

WALTZ

Slow

Now 'neath the sil - ver moon O - cean is glow - ing
O'er the calm bil - low Soft winds are blow - ing
Here bal - my bree - zes blow Pure joys in - vite us
And as we gent - ly row All things de - light us.
Hark how the sai - lor's cry Joy - ous - ly e - choes nigh:
San - ta Lu - ci - a! San - ta Lu - ci - a!

17

Sailing

Gavin Sunderland

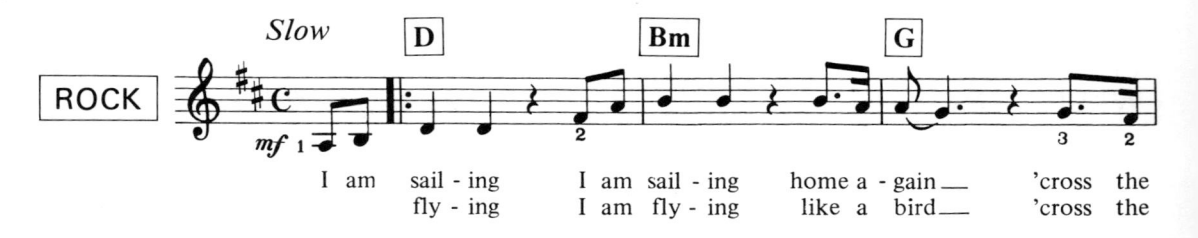

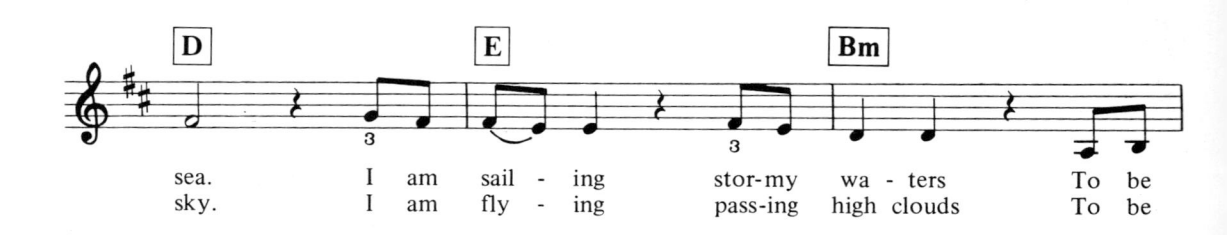

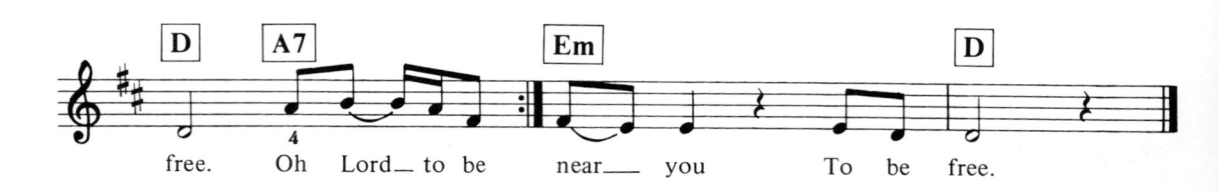

I am sail-ing I am sail-ing home a-gain 'cross the
fly-ing I am fly-ing like a bird 'cross the

sea. I am sail-ing stor-my wa-ters To be
sky. I am fly-ing pass-ing high clouds To be

near you to be free. I am Oh Lord to be near you To be
with you to be free. free.

free. Oh Lord to be near you To be free.

Londonderry Air

Traditional Irish

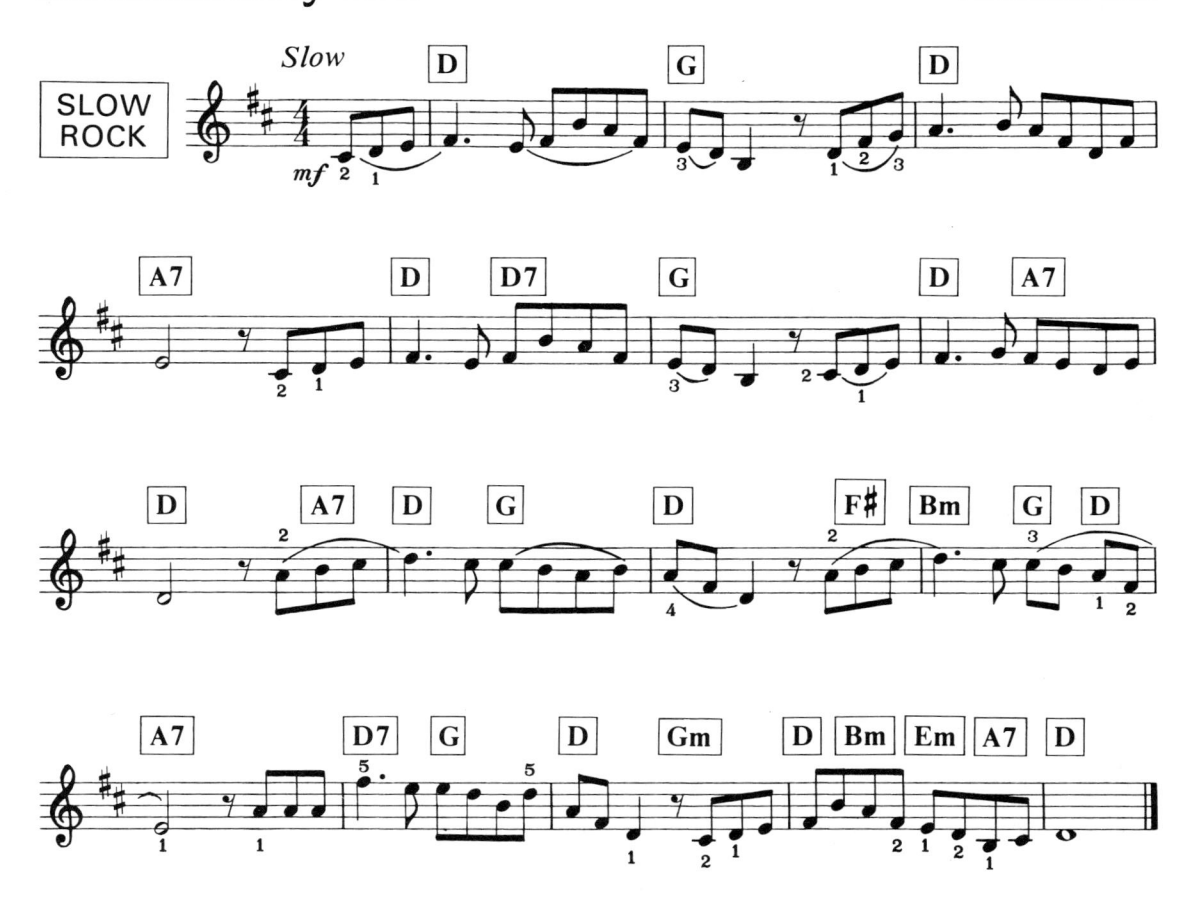

Shortnin' bread

Toreador's song

Bizet, arranged by Nick Haines

Meaty Beaty

Nick Haines

* Choose Fingered chord selector for the left hand part.

DISCO

FINGERED CHORD

Silent movie

Nick Haines

Blue note

Nick Haines

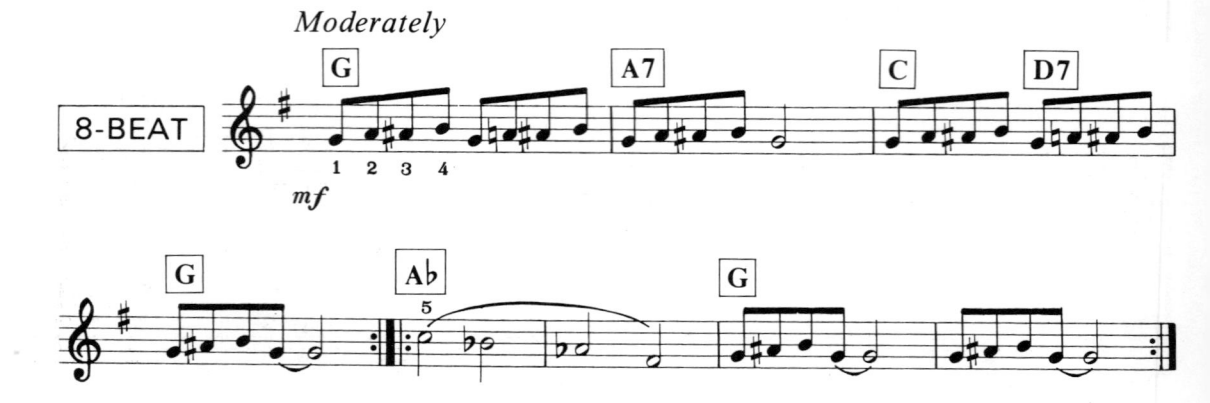

Coppelia

Delibes

In the hall of the Mountain King

(from Peer Gynt Suite)

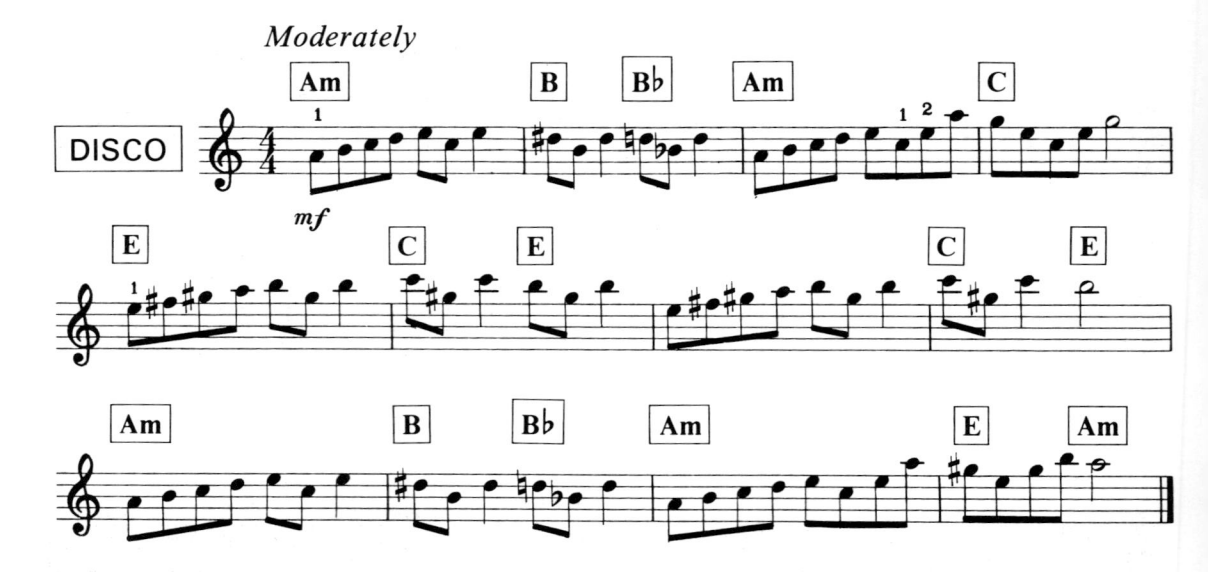

Grieg

Big Band Swinger

Nick Haines

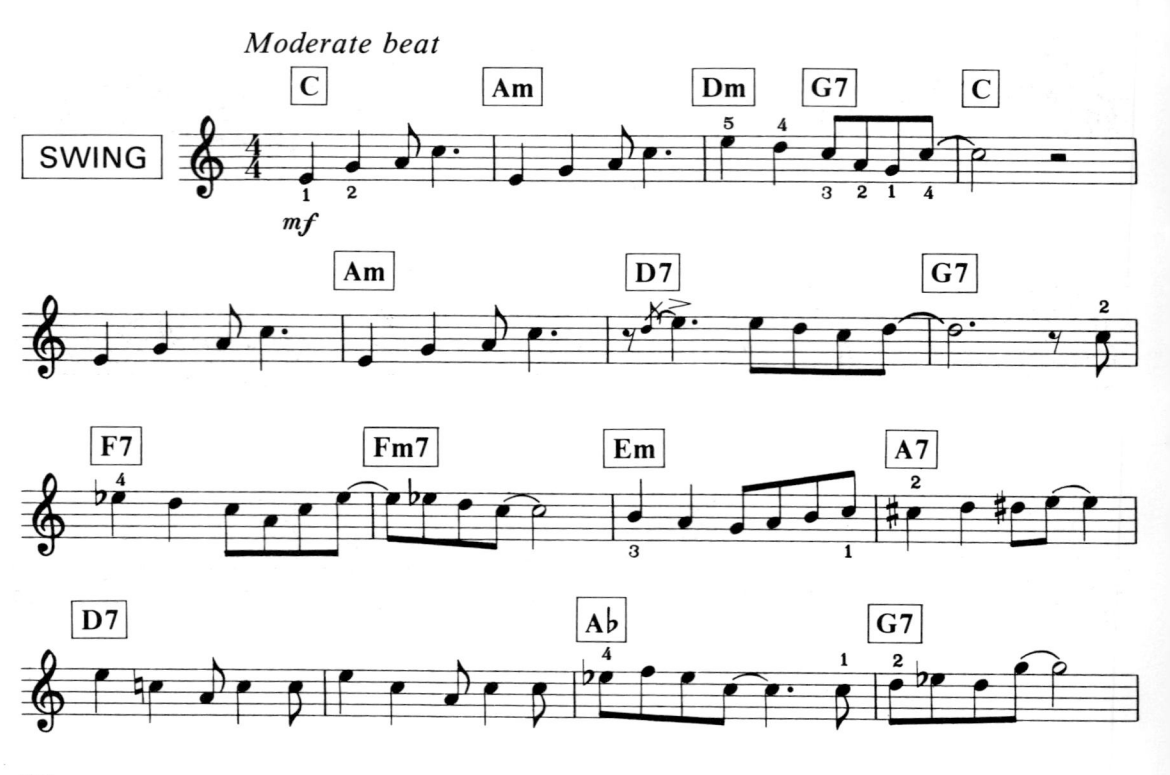

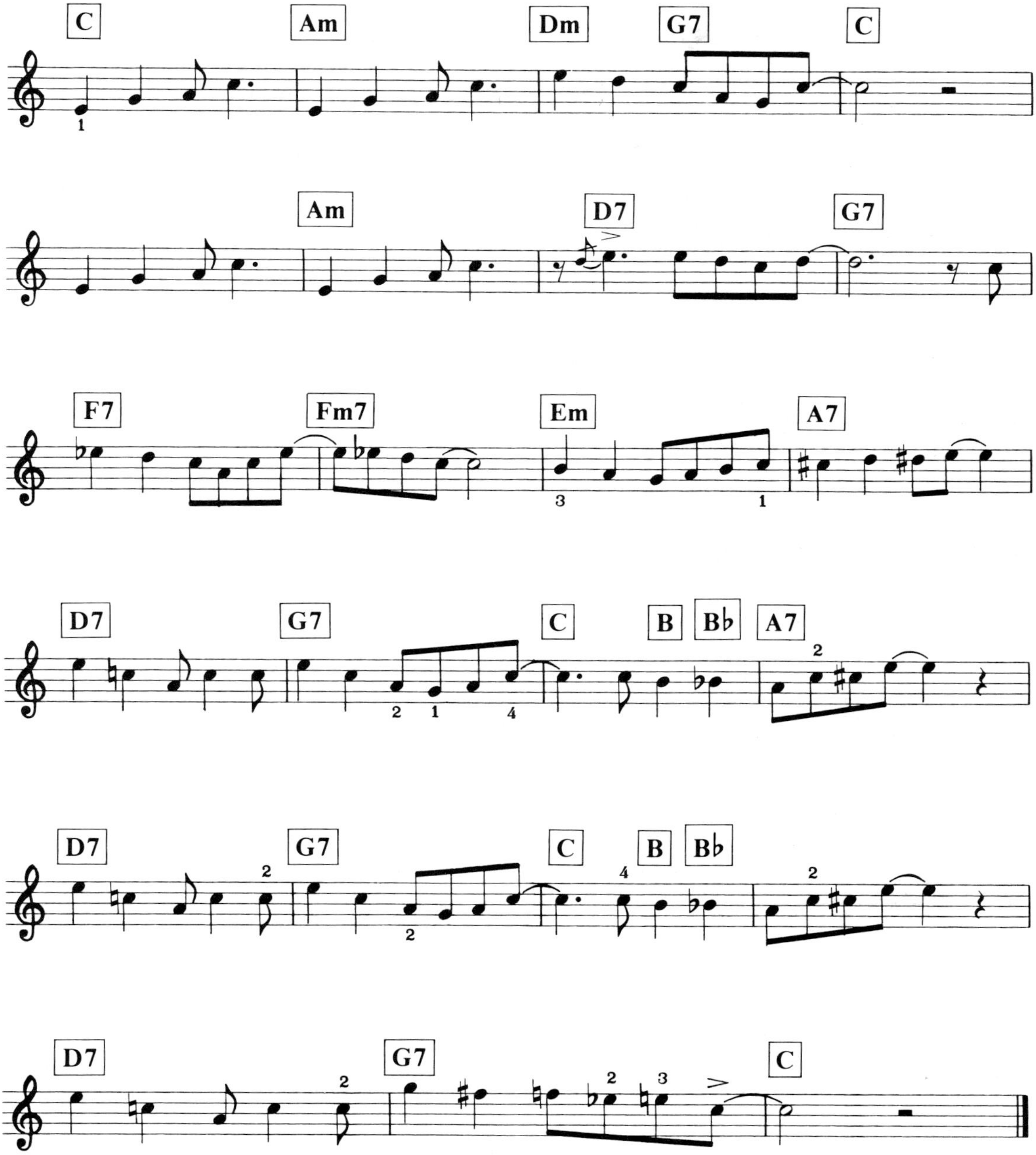
C Am Dm G7 C
Am D7 G7
F7 Fm7 Em A7
D7 G7 C B B♭ A7
D7 G7 C B B♭
D7 G7 C

The Entertainer

Scott Joplin, arranged by Nick Haines

Moderately

C C7 F Fm C C7
F D7 C D7 G7 C C
1 2
C7 F C G7 C
C7 F D7 G7
C C7 F E♭ C G7 C
C7 F Fm C G7 C

Eine kleine Nachtmusik

W. A. Mozart, arranged by Nick Haines